FUN WITH PHONE SOLICITORS
50 Ways to Get Even!

FUN WITH PHONE SOLICITORS

Fifty ways to get even!

ROBERT HARRIS

WARNER BOOKS

An AOL Time Warner Company

Warner Books, Inc., 1271 Avenue of the Americas, New York, NY 10020

Visit our Web site at www.twbookmark.com

For information on Time Warner Trade Publishing's online publishing program, visit www.ipublish.com.

 An AOL Time Warner Company

Printed in the United States of America

First Printing: October 2001

10 9 8 7 6 5 4 3 2 1

Library of Congress Cataloging-in-Publication Data

Harris, Robert W.
    Fun with phone solicitors : 50 ways to get even! / Robert Harris.
       p. cm.
    ISBN 0-446-67865-1
       1. Telephone selling I. Title.

  HF5438.3 .H37 2001
     658.8'4—dc21   2001026418
Cover design by Dan Pelavin
Cover and text illustrations by Dan Pelavin
Book design by H. Roberts Design

Author's Acknowledgments

I'd like to thank the following people: my agent, Jacques de Spoelberch, for finding the right publisher; Amy Einhorn and her colleagues at Warner for moving the book through the system quickly; H. Roberts Design and Dan Pelavin for the book design and clever illustrations; and Liz Petersen for her support and encouragement, and for suggesting the premise for *The Surrealism Subterfuge*.

A Note from the Author

It's a typical situation: You're enjoying dinner after a hard day's work when the phone rings. You answer, assuming it will be a friend. There's a pause, then a click, and then those dreaded words:

> "Good evening, may I speak to, uh, Mr. or Ms. [name pronounced incorrectly]?"

A solicitor! Yuk! What to do, what to do? Be polite? Get angry? Meekly hang up?

No, no, no! Be creative and enjoy yourself! All you need is *Fun with Phone Solicitors* to help you through such anxious moments.

Within these pages are fifty doctor-approved, environmentally friendly techniques that can help you deal effectively with those who annoy you the most. Techniques like "The Moron Maneuver," "The Inattention Interlude," and "The Just-the-Facts Jive" will leave pesky phone solicitors speechless, frustrated, and disoriented.

Each technique includes an example and some helpful tips. And each is rated with a degree of difficulty, from ☎ (the easiest) to ☎ ☎ ☎ ☎ ☎ (the most challenging), so Funsters of all skill levels can play! What's the key to success? Never get angry and never get frustrated (leave that to the solicitors). Oh, and never feel guilty.

For too long, phone solicitors have had the upper hand. Now it's time for us to stop being victims and fight back. I hope that the techniques in this book will inspire you to confront the problem of unwanted phone calls head-on. Remember: It's us against them. They barge into our homes uninvited, so forget the conventional rules of polite conversation and have some fun.

And in case you want to share one of your favorite techniques, you'll find a form in the back of the book for that purpose. Who knows—maybe your technique will be featured in the next edition of *Fun with Phone Solicitors*!

A Brief History of Phone Solicitation

On the afternoon of March 12, 1876, Alexander Graham Bell, who bore a striking resemblance to actor Don Ameche, invented the telephone. At approximately 7:12 that evening, while eating dinner, he received a "courtesy call" from a local dry-cleaning establishment. Thus began the contentious relationship between telephone owner and telephone solicitor.

Since that fateful day, solicitors have attempted to sell anything and everything over the phone. But for many decades, their efforts were hampered by limitations in the available equipment. Even at the midpoint of the twentieth century, numbers still had to be dialed by hand on rotary phones, thus making it difficult to victimize more than a small segment of the population. So as the halcyon Eisenhower years drew to a close, most polite citizens were unaware of the potential threat to their peace of mind.

The 1960s brought unrest, rebellion, and questionable fashion to our nation. One constant, however, was the persistence of phone solicitors. But the number of solicitors actually declined, according to experts. However, because of extensive use of recreational drugs during that decade, there's just no way to be sure exactly what was going on.

In the 1970s, at the dawn of the computer age, phone solicitors got a real boost. Computerized phone directories and automatic-dialing machines made it possible to annoy the maximum number of people with minimum effort. Phone solicitors became giddy with power, and their telemarketing strategies took on a new aggressiveness. Mr. and Mrs. Suburbia were starting to get annoyed.

Even with the advantages of the new technology, phone solicitors still had trouble convincing average folks to part with their hard-earned money. In fact, from 1979 to 1999, only seven cold calls actually resulted in some kind of sale. Nevertheless, phone solicitors persist. This tendency to ignore reality and press ahead toward an unreachable goal in the face of extreme opposition is known as *Solicitor Syndrome*. The details of the malady are well understood in the psychiatric community, but, unfortunately, space does not permit us to explore that topic in the present work.

Over the years, average citizens have tried to resist pesky phone solicitors with a variety of responses. During the 1970s, it was "No thank you." During the 1980s, the preferred phrase was "I'm not interested at this time." The 1990s saw nearly equal use of two responses: "Please don't call again" and "G——it, not another f—— solicitor!" And around the turn of the century, the most common response to uninvited callers became "You lousy jerk, I'm trying to watch *Who Wants to Be a Millionaire*!"

Today we are amused by these clumsy attempts to deter phone solicitors. We now know that modern Fun techniques are the only effective tools for fending off annoying sales pitches. Although not 100 percent reliable, they are humanity's best hope for combating obnoxious phone solicitors.

The power of the Fun method lies in its simplicity: It shifts the irritation from the callee to the caller, and also provides an outlet for creative expression. So instead of responding to the phone's ring with apprehension, Funsters actually welcome calls, seeing them as opportunities to waste a solicitor's time and energy.

Perhaps there will come a day when phone calls are made only by friends, family members, and business associates. But until that day comes, we must remain vigilant. An unwanted call could come at any time on any day, so we must be ready to act. If each person tried to have just a little Fun with phone solicitors, imagine what a difference it would make. To paraphrase Lincoln: "The world will little note, nor long remember, what phone solicitors say here, but it can never forget what Funsters did here."

FUN WITH PHONE SOLICITORS
50 Ways to Get Even!

The Receptionist Ruse

DEGREE OF DIFFICULTY

TECHNIQUE: Elude the solicitor's pitch by transferring him via an imaginary inter-office telephone system.

E X A M P L E

SOLICITOR: "Good afternoon—I'm calling for Ms. Beale."

FUNSTER: "One moment please—I'll connect you." [*Press two buttons in sequence on your phone.*]

After about five seconds, expect the solicitor to say something like "Hello—is anyone there?" Ask for whom he's holding, then press the phone buttons again. At this point the game will probably be over. It's highly unlikely that it will go to a third round—but one can dream, can't one?

The Middleman Misdirection

DEGREE OF DIFFICULTY

TECHNIQUE: Disrupt the solicitor's rhythm by relaying his offer to an imaginary friend in another room.

EXAMPLE

SOLICITOR: "Good evening—have I reached Mrs. McCormick?"

FUNSTER: "Yes."

S: "I represent the Acme Hotel and Spa in Orlando, and I—"

F: [*Very loudly aside*] "HUH? . . . [*Pause*] . . . HE SAYS HE REPRESENTS THE ACME HOTEL AND SPA!"

S: "I'm calling tonight to make you a special offer."

F: "HE SAYS HE'S CALLING TO MAKE A SPECIAL OFFER!"

S: "Uh, well, we'd like you to be our guest for a weekend, and—"

F: "HE WANTS ME TO BE HIS GUEST FOR A WEEKEND!"

S: "Ma'am, is this a bad time?"

S: [*Solicitor hangs up.*]

BONUS POINTS: If the solicitor refuses to give in after a few rounds, you can end the conversation by saying "I really have to go. I'm getting tired of yelling."

This one will be more effective if you can get some of the facts slightly wrong as you relay them. Doing so will keep the solicitor engaged, and he'll try harder.

The Put-Down Ploy

TECHNIQUE: Avoid the solicitor by just putting the phone down and walking away.

EXAMPLE

SOLICITOR: "Good afternoon—is this Mr. Roger Davis?"

FUNSTER: "Yes."

S: "My name is Sally, and I'm calling—"

F: [*Quietly put the phone down and continue with your life.*]

S: [*Solicitor hangs up.*]

At first you'll probably listen for the solicitor's attempts to get a response from you. Although this can be amusing, it really defeats the purpose of the technique. So just try to continue with what you were doing before you were so rudely interrupted.

For full credit, it's essential that you get the *solicitor* to end the "conversation." So be sure to wait at least thirty seconds before you come back and hang up.

The Answering-Machine Antic

TECHNIQUE: Sidestep a conversation with the solicitor by simulating an answering machine greeting.

EXAMPLE

SOLICITOR: "Hello, this is Darnell with The Acme Group. May I speak with Mr. or Mrs.—"

FUNSTER: "Hello, you've reached the Franklin residence. At the tone, please leave a brief message, and we'll get back to you." [*Make a beep sound or press a button on your phone and hold it down for a couple of seconds.*]

S: [*Solicitor hangs up.*]

Chances are good that the solicitor will hang up before you can finish. But if he does try to leave a message, cut him off after a few seconds with a *beep-beep*, and then hang up.

The Order-Line Obfuscation

DEGREE OF DIFFICULTY

TECHNIQUE: Dodge the solicitor's pitch by guiding her to the correct department within your organization.

EXAMPLE

SOLICITOR: "Good evening—is this, uh, Mr. Pruitt?"

FUNSTER: "Speaking—go ahead with your order."

S: "Uh—well, Mr. Pruitt, I'm Yvonne at Acme Business Solutions. We're conducting a survey of—"

F: "No, no, lady—this line is for orders only. I think you want Customer Service. Do you want Customer Service?"

S: "I'm sorry. I must have dialed the wrong number."

F: "Yeah, like I said, this line is for orders only. . . ."

If the solicitor asks what company she's reached, make up some official-sounding name, like "Consolidated Import and Export" or "Worldwide Amalgamated."

And if she tries to be difficult by requesting the Customer Service number, just give her your number with the last two digits reversed, or your number with a 1–800 in front of it.

The Teenager Transfer

TECHNIQUE: Nettle the solicitor by calling his intended victim in the manner of a typical self-absorbed fourteen-year-old.

E X A M P L E

SOLICITOR: "Hello—may I please speak with Mrs. Ruskin?"

FUNSTER: "Hang on." [*As loudly as possible*] **"MOMMMMM!"** [*Toss the phone down and walk away.*]

After seven or eight seconds, pick up the phone and say "Hello?" If the solicitor is still on the line, he will probably say "Yes, I was holding for Mrs. Ruskin." At this point you might feel a bit of guilt for taking advantage of the solicitor's naïveté, but do not weaken—press onward nevertheless. Yell "Mom!" at the top of your lungs once again.

The Is-Anyone-There Initiative

DEGREE OF DIFFICULTY

TECHNIQUE: Head off interaction with the solicitor by simply not being able to hear him.

E X A M P L E

SOLICITOR: "Good evening. May I speak to, uh, Mr. or Mrs. Brown?"

FUNSTER: "Hello?"

S : "Yes, I'm Mr. Ramirez calling from Acme—"

F: "Hel-*lo?* Is anyone there?"

S : "Yes sir, I'm calling about—"

F: [*Impatiently*] "Is—any—one—there?"

S : "Yes sir, can you hear—"

F: [*Angrily*] "Now look, whoever you are, I'm not playing your little game. What's next? Heavy breathing?"

S : [*Solicitor hangs up.*]

To make this technique work, be sure to talk over the solicitor to give the impression that you can't hear him.

And since this one probably won't last for very long, it's important to get ticked off pretty early in the encounter. But if the solicitor does persist, you can start speculating about who the crank caller is. (For example: "Uncle Frank—is that you again? It's not funny anymore!")

The Bad-Connection Bamboozlement

DEGREE OF DIFFICULTY

TECHNIQUE: Throw off the solicitor's rhythm by forcing him to speak more loudly than normal.

E X A M P L E

SOLICITOR: "Good evening. Have I reached the Umstead home?"

FUNSTER: "What? Umstead? Yes, I'm Lance Umstead."

S: "Hi Mr. Umstead, I'm calling from—"

F: "We must have a bad connection. I can barely hear you." [*Hold the receiver away from your ear to avoid damage to your hearing.*]

S: "MR. UMSTEAD, I'M CALLING FROM ACME RESORTS IN MYRTLE BEACH, SOUTH CAROLINA."

F: "Where? Please speak up."

S: "MYRTLE BEACH, SOUTH CAROLINA!"

F: **"What beach was that?"**

S: "MYRTLE BEACH. M–Y–R–T–L–E!"

F: **"No, no—you've got the wrong number. I don't live any-
where near Myrtle Beach." [*Hang up*.]**

Timing is the key to success here. If you go
one step too far, the solicitor will be the first to
hang up and you'll receive only partial credit.
And be sure not to raise *your* voice—the problem
is on the *other* end of the line!

The Wrong-Number Wrangle

DEGREE OF DIFFICULTY

TECHNIQUE: Rattle the solicitor with some confusion about just what number was dialed.

E X A M P L E

SOLICITOR: "Good evening, uh, Ms. Parker? This is Miss D'Angelo, calling for Acme Video of the Month Club."

FUNSTER: "I think you might have misdialed. What number were you trying to reach?"

S : "I thought I dialed 555–4321."

F : "Oh, no—this is 555-4-3-2-1." [*Emphasize the last two digits, saying them slowly.*]

S : "Well, that's what I just said: 555–4321."

F : "What? Say the number again."

S : "555–4321. Is this not Ms.—"

F : "Oh *555*-4321? [*Emphasize the first three digits.*] "No, no, we don't use that number anymore."

S: "Well, just what *is* your number?"

F: **"Oh, I'm sorry, my number's unlisted."**

S: [*Solicitor hangs up.*]

With this technique you'll want to be as sincere and helpful as possible. You're just trying to get the solicitor to where she wants to go.

And when it comes time to end the conversation, use your imagination. Here are a few other possibilities:

- "Oh, I'm sorry, my number's been disconnected."
- "Come to think of it, I don't believe I *have* a number."
- "It's been *years* since I've had a number!"
- Or just say the number differently: "This is 'five-fifty-five, forty-three, twenty-one.'"

The Paranoia Pretense

TECHNIQUE: Distract the solicitor with jittery "Us vs. Them" concerns.

E X A M P L E

SOLICITOR: "Good evening—am I speaking with Mr. Elmore?"

FUNSTER: "I'm listening."

S : "Oh, uh, well. My name is Ed Gibson, and I represent the Acme Financial Group."

F: "Is that some kind of foreign left-wing organization?"

S : "No sir, nothing like that. Anyway, I'm calling tonight to offer you a free gift. We'd like to send you—"

F: "Are you recording this call?"

S : "Uh, well, no, of course not. As I was saying, we'd like to send you a complimentary copy of our monthly newsletter that—"

F: "They're coming, aren't they?"

S : "Who? Who's coming?"

F: **"Wait—did you hear that?"**

S: "Hear what, sir?"

Ideally, the solicitor will give up after a few rounds. But if he hangs on, be prepared to go all out: imaginary friends, assassination plots, aliens, et cetera.

BONUS POINTS: See if you can work the phrase "Big Brother" into the conversation.

The Dysfunctional-Family Deception

TECHNIQUE: Forestall the solicitor by drawing him into a weird domestic situation.

EXAMPLE

SOLICITOR: "Good afternoon. Is this Ms. Smith?"

FUNSTER: "Yes."

S: "This is a courtesy call from Acme Photography, your neighborhood family portrait studio."

F: "Yes, what can I—*No, Suzy! Put Daddy's power drill down!*—I'm sorry. You were saying?"

S: "Uh—I'm calling with a special offer."

F: "*Play with those matches outside, young man!*—I do apologize. Now, you said something about an offer?"

S: "Yes ma'am. We're having a sale on our popular—"

F: *"No, TV first and* **then** *homework. You know the rules.—* You're having a sale?"

S: "Yes ma'am. For the next two weeks, we're offering—"

F: *"No, that's drain opener,* **not Kool-Aid. Now put it back in the cabinet.—I'm sorry, what was that last part?"**

S: [*Solicitor hangs up.*]

This technique really puts the "fun" back in "dysfunctional"! Here are some other possible admonitions to the kids:

- "That's not the way you make a hangman's noose. Now go to your room and practice."
- "No, we're not going to shave the dog. Today's not Saturday!"
- "Don't walk in that broken glass—what's wrong with you?"
- "No, don't worry, he's not dead. Hamsters just sleep a lot."

17

The Flag-Waver Flimflam

DEGREE OF DIFFICULTY

TECHNIQUE: Disorient the solicitor with a dose of hard-core right-wing patriotism.

EXAMPLE

SOLICITOR: "Hi, could I speak to Virgil Lawson?"

FUNSTER: "That's *Colonel* Lawson, retired."

S: "Yes, well, Colonel Lawson, I'm calling tonight with a special offer from Acme Vinyl Siding."

F: "Buy American, that's my motto. None of that cheap overseas crap in this house."

S: "Well, our product is made right here in America by skilled craftsmen."

F: "You don't employ any of those illegals, do you? No room for slackers here in the U. S. of A."

S: "No sir, of course not. Now, I—"

F: "Love it or leave it, you know what I mean?"

S: "Well, sir, right now we're offering one window free with every three windows purchased. How does that sound?"

F: **"Things weren't free in Normandy, were they, my friend?"**

S: "Sir?"

There's a fine line between patriotism and strangeness, and this is your chance to cross it. If the solicitor doesn't bail out quickly, just start a tirade about liberalism and he'll soon hang up.

BONUS POINTS: Say either "America, right or wrong!" or "First Amendment my a—!" during the conversation.

The Singsong Sidestep

DEGREE OF DIFFICULTY

TECHNIQUE: Dumbfound the solicitor by singing your responses.

EXAMPLE

SOLICITOR: "Hello, could I please speak with Ms. Carson?"

FUNSTER: [*Singing*] "Thiiiiis is Pau-la Carrr-sonnnn."

S: "Well, Ms. Carson, my name's Tamira, and I'm calling with an offer from Acme Telecom."

F: [*Singing*] **"Tell mee allll about it!"**

S: "Well, you're certainly in a good mood this evening. Now ma'am, may I ask if you're currently using a cellular phone to make your long-distance calls?"

F: [*Singing*] **"Noooo, I don't haaaave a cell phone!"**

Start out by just giving your normal speech a little melodic variation, then get more and more operatic as you go along. If the solicitor persists, you might have to break into a real song, like "Three Blind Mice," "Row Row Row Your Boat," or "America the Beautiful."

And if the solicitor ever asks why you're singing, just sing "To staaay in prac-tice, of course!"

The Drop-the-Phone Drill

DEGREE OF DIFFICULTY

TECHNIQUE: Stave off the solicitor's pitch by dropping the phone again and again.

E X A M P L E

SOLICITOR: "Good evening—have I reached the O'Brien residence?"

FUNSTER: "Yes. Who's calling?"

S: "I represent Acme Home Mortgage Corporation."

F: [*Drop the phone.*] **"Sorry."**

S: "That's all right. Now, I'm calling tonight to see if I could interest you in—"

F: [*Drop the phone.*] **"Sorry. Dang phone! Now, you were saying?"**

S: "Uh, well, I'd like to offer you, with no obligation, a—"

F: [*Drop the phone.*] **"Gee, I feel like such a . . . [*Drop the phone.*] . . . darn it!"**

S: [*Solicitor hangs up.*]

The trick here is to see how many drops you can execute before the solicitor hangs up. Start with two and work your way up gradually. Don't aim too high too fast.

BONUS POINTS: If you're really adventurous, try increasing the severity of your expletives as you go along. You'll be glad you did.

The Simpleton Strategy

DEGREE OF DIFFICULTY

TECHNIQUE: Perplex the solicitor with a conversation that suggests you have the IQ of a turnip.

E X A M P L E

SOLICITOR: "Good evening—is this Ms. Suzanne Fisher?"

FUNSTER: "Uh, wait a sec—yeah, that's me."

S: "I'm Mr. Gregson calling from Acme Asphalt Company—we're specialists in home driveway paving."

F: "Driveway? That's where my husband parks the car!"

S: "Yes, ma'am. And since your car is one of your largest investments—"

F: "It's a real nice car. It's blue. We go for rides!"

S: "Uh—well, our company offers free estimates and a five-year limited warranty. Now, our representatives will be in your area tomorrow, and—"

F: "Tomorrow is the day after today!"

S: "Ma'am?"

F: "Today is the day after yesterday!"

S: [*Solicitor hangs up.*]

To pull this one off, just imagine you had a frontal lobotomy when you were five and you've done nothing but watch TV ever since. And make sure there's a certain glee in your voice (for coming up with what you think are appropriate responses).

The Born-Yesterday Bluff

TECHNIQUE: Demoralize the solicitor with astounding naïveté.

E X A M P L E

SOLICITOR: "Good evening—Mr. Gabriel?"

FUNSTER: **"Yes, that's me."**

S: "Sir, I'm calling from Acme Consolidated Financial in Chicago."

F: **"Chicago? You mean outside New York?"**

S: "No sir. Chicago. Chicago, Illinois."

F: **"Oh."**

S: "Well, Mr. Gabriel, you've been selected to receive our new Gold/Silver credit card."

F: **"Credit card? How's that work?"**

S: "Sir?"

F: **"The credit card thing. How's it work?"**

S: "Like any card, it allows you to structure your payments for purchases like furniture and appliances."

F: "That's news to me. And by 'furniture' you mean . . . ?"

S: "Uh—well, furniture. Or other items for your home. You may have seen our advertisement on TV."

F: "TV? What do you mean?"

S: "On the TV. Our ad with the former heavyweight champ. Maybe you saw it during the Super Bowl."

F: "Super *what*?"

The idea is to take the solicitor as far away as possible from his reason for calling. Of course, he'll return to the reason soon enough. But when that happens, just start the process over, asking the same types of inane questions.

The Verbatim Variation

DEGREE OF DIFFICULTY

TECHNIQUE: Annoy the solicitor by repeating everything she says.

EXAMPLE

SOLICITOR: "Hello, could I, uh, speak to Mr. Delgado?"

FUNSTER: "Yes, Mr. Delgado."

S: "I'm Ms. Cantrell, and this is a courtesy call from Acme Security Systems."

F: "Acme Security Systems."

S: "Yes, and I'm calling tonight with a limited-time offer."

F: "Limited-time offer."

S: "That's right. From now until the end of the month, we're offering free installation on any of our premium systems."

F: "Free installation."

S: "Yes. Now, can I arrange an appointment?"

F: "Arrange an appointment."

S: "Uh—sir, am I making myself clear?"

F: **"Making myself clear."**

This technique takes a while, but it requires very little effort. You should start out uninvolved, using a monotone.

BONUS POINTS: As the conversation goes along, try to sound more and more like a parrot.

The Moron Maneuver

DEGREE OF DIFFICULTY

TECHNIQUE: Frustrate the solicitor with an exceptional inability to grasp the facts.

E X A M P L E

SOLICITOR: "Hello, may I speak to Mr. or Mrs. Williams?"

FUNSTER: "This is Mr. Williams."

S: "This is Ms. Santos with Acme Home Improvement Products. How are you this evening?"

F: "Hackney?"

S: "No sir—Acme. And I'm calling tonight to tell you about our spring special on gutters."

F: "Springs? I don't think I need any springs."

S: "Oh, no sir, it's a spring sale—on our premium aluminum gutters. Now, we're prepared to offer you free installation with any purchase before the end of the month."

F: "So let me get this straight. You're selling gutters with springs, and the first month is free?"

S: "No sir, the installation is—I mean, the gutters are—let me explain."

F: **"Okay, but what do aluminum gutters have to do with acne?"**

S: "Acme. The name is Acme. A–C–M–E. Now if I could just . . ."

The trick here is not to overplay your stupidity. Remember, it's the *solicitor's* fault you don't understand.

Bonus Points: Pat yourself on the back for a job well done if the solicitor apologizes for not being clear enough.

And if the solicitor refuses to give in, just say "This is *way* too complicated for someone like me" and hang up.

The Inattention Interlude

TECHNIQUE: Nullify the solicitor's pitch by not paying attention.

E X A M P L E

SOLICITOR: "Hi, could I speak to Mr. Gorman?"

FUNSTER: "This is Fred Gorman."

S: "Mr. Gorman, I'm calling from Acme Bank and Trust of St. Louis. Because of your outstanding credit record, we're pleased to offer you, without cost or obligation, our new platinum card. Now, the card has a credit limit of $5,000 and a low introductory rate of only 6.3 percent. And if you accept our offer this evening, I'm also authorized to include our free booklet, *Managing Your Dollars.*"

F: *[Silence]*

S: "Sir? Are you there?

F: "Huh? What was that?"

If the solicitor tries to get away with repeating just the last sentence, say "No, before that." And if that doesn't get the desired response, be prepared to say "No, no. I said 'This is Fred Gorman,' and then *you* said—what?"

BONUS POINTS: Once you get the hang of this one, you might want to try the advanced version (degree of difficulty =  ☎ ☎ ☎ ☎). Here, after the solicitor *repeats* the pitch, you once again say "Huh? What was that?" Then expect an unkind comment about your mother.

33

The Doggie-Talk Dodge

DEGREE OF DIFFICULTY

☎ ☎

TECHNIQUE: Fluster the solicitor by dividing your attention between her and your loyal companion.

E X A M P L E

SOLICITOR: "Good evening—am I speaking with Ms. Felicia Judd?"

FUNSTER: "Yes, this is—*Scruffy! Get down!*—yes, this is Ms. Judd. Who's calling?"

S: "Ms. Judd, this is Beverly with a courtesy call from Acme Heating Systems. As you know, winter will soon be upon us."

F: "Oh, I know. There's already a nip in the—*Yes, I know. Mommy wuvs you too!*"

S: "Uh—so we're offering our deluxe furnace inspection and tune-up to homeowners in your neighborhood. Can we schedule an appointment?"

F: **"Well, I'm—*Yes, who's a good dog? Hmm? Who's a good doggie? Such a good doggie!*—I'm not so sure."**

S: "Our work is guaranteed for ninety days, and—"

F: **"So you're saying—*Scruffy! No, not the remote! Scruffy!*—I'm sorry. Uh, what company are you with?"**

Even if the solicitor is a dog lover, this one will drive her nuts. At some point it will become apparent that there's just no way to hold your attention when your precious pet is around, and the solicitor will cut her losses and move on.

The Laughter Lampoon

DEGREE OF DIFFICULTY

TECHNIQUE: Hold off the solicitor by experiencing an uncontrollable case of the giggles.

EXAMPLE

SOLICITOR: "Hello—may I please speak to Mr. or Mrs. White?"

FUNSTER: [*Laugh*] "This . . . this is Tim . . . [*Giggle*] . . . White."

S: "Mr. White, the reason I'm calling is to offer you a free trial subscription to *Money Money Money*, the award-winning financial newsletter."

F: [*Laugh*] "Well . . . I've never . . . [*Guffaw*] . . . heard of . . . [*Snicker*] . . . that newsletter."

S: "It's one of the best resources for those who like to manage their own investments."

F: [*Chuckle*] "I . . . do my . . . [*Laugh*] . . . own investing . . . [*Titter*]"

S: "Well, Mr. White, would you like to take advantage of this opportunity?"

F: [*Chortle*] "I . . . I . . . [*Giggle*] . . . I really . . . [*Laugh uncontrollably*]"

S: [*Solicitor hangs up.*]

Once the solicitor realizes that your mind is on something other than the conversation, he'll probably bail out without so much as a "goodbye." But if he hangs on and eventually asks "What's so funny?" just become so amused that you can't even get out an answer, and continue laughing until the solicitor hangs up.

The Impatience Improvisation

DEGREE OF DIFFICULTY

Technique: Exasperate the solicitor by eagerly helping to finish his sentences.

EXAMPLE

Solicitor: "Hello. Have I reached Ms.—"

Funster: "Brown. Yes, that's me."

S: "I'm Mr. Cox, and I represent—"

F: "XYZ Mortgage Company?"

S: "Uh, no. Acme Telephone Company. I'm calling to offer you—"

F: "Call forwarding?"

S: "Uh, well, no. A customized calling plan. And the cost is only—"

F: "Four dollars a month?"

S: "No, no. The cost is—"

F: **"Two dollars a month?"**

S: "Ma'am, if I could just—"

F: **"Find true love?"**

The key to this technique is to sustain the interruptions until the solicitor either sighs with frustration or creates a clever combination of the conventional four-letter words. Then say "Well, if you're going to take *that* tone," and hang up.

The Yada-Yada Yammer

DEGREE OF DIFFICULTY

☎ ☎ ☎

TECHNIQUE: Weaken the impact of the solicitor's offer by helpfully moving the conversation along.

E X A M P L E

SOLICITOR: "Hi, could I speak to Mr. or Mrs. Allen?"

FUNSTER: "Yeah, sure, I'm Bill Allen."

S: "I hope I haven't called at a bad time."

F: "No, no. I know you're just doing your job, and you've got to make a living, yada-yada-yada."

S: "Well, I won't take much of your time. My name is Jack Mooney, and I represent the Acme Home Refinancing Corporation. As a homeowner, you probably—"

F: "Sure, sure, I've got it: There's some special rate, and some deal on closing costs, yada-yada-yada."

S: "Well, yes. Now, if I could just explain our offer. You see, we—"

F: **"Oh, I understand. You want to get some basic informa-tion, and then send me some literature, yada-yada-yada."**

S: "Well, there's a bit more to it than that. Now if I may—"

F: **"I know, I know, you want to tell me some of the details, and then get my address, yada-yada-yada."**

The goal here is to make sure you never give the solicitor the chance to convey any particulars about his offer. You've heard it all before, and you certainly don't want to hear it again now.

The Riddle Rattle

DEGREE OF DIFFICULTY

TECHNIQUE: Brighten the solicitor's day with a riddle or joke, then demand the same from him.

E X A M P L E

SOLICITOR: "Good afternoon—Ms. Olsen?"

FUNSTER: "Yes, this is Ms. Olsen."

S: "My name is Mr. Sellars, and I'm with Acme Time-Share Getaways. How are you today?"

F: "Hey, do you want to hear a good joke?"

S: "Uh, well, sure."

F: "Okay. Knock-knock."

S: "Who's there?"

F: "Impatient cow."

S: "All right, impatient c—"

F: "Moooooo!"

S: "That's pretty good. Now, the reason for my call is—"

F: **"Hey, wait a minute. It's your turn."**

S: "Ma'am?"

F: **[*Insistently*] "I told *you* a joke, now you have to tell *me* one."**

The solicitor will probably refuse to play, since he's obviously not making much headway with his sales pitch. But if he does give in and come up with a joke, just say with a sneer "That's not very funny" or "I've heard that one before" and hang up.

Bonus Points: Use a joke that's really not very funny and see if the solicitor laughs anyway in a pathetic effort to please you.

The Cliché Charade

TECHNIQUE: Stun the solicitor with a series of banal, overused expressions that lead nowhere.

E X A M P L E

SOLICITOR: "Hello, is this Mr. Armstrong?"

FUNSTER: "That's me—if I'm lyin', I'm dyin'. Who's this?"

S: "Good evening, sir. I'm Kesha with Acme Window Replacement Service. How are you this evening?"

F: "Fit as a fiddle!"

S: "Well sir, I'm calling with a limited-time offer."

F: **"Time is money, they say."**

S: "That's right. And many people don't know that old, loose-fitting windows are really costing them money."

F: **"When it rains, it pours—that's my view."**

S: "Uh, yes sir. Now, if we could just schedule an appointment for a free, no-obligation estimate."

F: **"Tomorrow's another day."**

S: "Sir?"

At first, try to make the cliché fit the conversation. But after a few exchanges, it really won't matter. Just use whatever comes to mind, and let the solicitor figure it out!

Here are some other choice clichés to consider using:

- "Time flies."
- "If you're failing to plan, you're planning to fail."
- "What goes around comes around."
- "No pain, no gain."
- "It's always darkest before the dawn."
- "A rolling stone gathers no moss."

45

The Down-and-Out Deflection

DEGREE OF DIFFICULTY

TECHNIQUE: Disconcert the solicitor by letting him know just how bad things are in your life.

E X A M P L E

SOLICITOR: "Hello, may I please speak with Mr. Johnson?"

FUNSTER: **"Oh, I suppose. I've got nothing better to do."**

S: "How are you this evening, sir?"

F: **[*Sadly*] "Well, I'm kinda bummed. I was fired today. But that's not your problem. What can I do for you?"**

S: "I'm calling from Acme Quick Claim Insurance, and if you'll give me just two minutes—"

F: **[*Incredulously*] "And the *market*! Why did I buy those dot-com stocks? But you were saying?"**

S: "Yes sir. You see, our company offers the lowest car insurance rates in the business, guaranteed."

F: [*With frustration*] "It's just that you try and try and try, but nothing seems to go your way."

S: "I'm sorry to hear that, sir. But by saving money on your car insurance, you will—"

F: "And today at lunch my wallet was stolen."

Life can be rough at times, and this is one of those times. Share your hardships with the solicitor until he comes to realize that this isn't the best time to be bothering you.

Some other possible causes of despair are:

- "I can't find *The Love Boat* reruns on any channel."
- "My daughter needs *another* brain operation."
- "The air-conditioner is on the fritz."
- "And my doctor said those tests I took last week were inconclusive."

The Grief Gaffe

DEGREE OF DIFFICULTY

TECHNIQUE: Subdue the solicitor by disclosing your recent loss of the intended victim.

EXAMPLE

SOLICITOR: "Good evening, may I speak to Donald Jenkins?"

FUNSTER: "I'm afraid—well, he's . . . [*Have trouble speaking*] . . . no longer . . . with us."

S: "Oh, my condolences."

F: "Thank you. It's just that it was so unexpected. I mean, to be torn apart by a grizzly bear—in his own bedroom! Oh, what will I do without him?"

S: [*Solicitor hangs up.*]

If for some reason, the solicitor doesn't hang up, just break down and sob and wail uncontrollably until she gives in.

Here are some other possible causes of untimely demise:

- "He laughed himself to death during a rerun of *Hogan's Heroes*. Boy, did he love that John Banner."
- "He just had to save money and buy that *used* bungee cord."
- "He fell into one of those tree-limb chippers."
- "He donated blood once too often. Always thinking of others!"

The Senility Scenario

DEGREE OF DIFFICULTY
☎ ☎ ☎

TECHNIQUE: Undermine the solicitor's efforts with responses that suggest you're about one brick short of a load.

EXAMPLE

SOLICITOR: "Good evening. Is this Mr. Mark Walker?"

FUNSTER: "That's me, all right. Yep, I'm here. Present and accounted for!"

S: "Well, Mr. Walker, I'm calling with a special offer from Acme Home Financing Corporation."

F: "What day is this?"

S: "Uh—it's Thursday, the 25th. Now, as you know, the economy is slowing down, and interest rates are unpredictable."

F: "Well, my memory's not as good as it used to be."

S: "The truth is, this is probably the best time to refinance."

F: "That Reagan's doing a great job!"

S: "Sir?"

F: **"Now I've got it!"**

S: "Sir?"

For this technique, be sure to use an animated, happy voice. The idea is to give the impression that you either took a blow to the head or you've been forgetting your medication—but that you couldn't care less.

If you go blank at any point and can't come up with anything to say, just repeat one of your previous statements. Or you could blurt out some unexpected word or phrase like "Incoming!" or "I can't find my glasses."

The Hard-Sell Hoax

DEGREE OF DIFFICULTY

TECHNIQUE: Build an impenetrable wall between yourself and the solicitor with skepticism, cynicism, and mistrust.

E X A M P L E

SOLICITOR: "Hello, have I reached Ms. Lambert?"

FUNSTER: [*Suspiciously*] **"Uhhhh—do I know you?"**

S: "No ma'am. I'm Mr. Lyle, and I represent the Acme Music and Video Club."

F: **"Yeah, *sure* you do."**

S: "Yes ma'am. And I'm calling to make you a special offer that I'm sure you'll appreciate."

F: **"An offer? I doubt *that*."**

S: "Uh, well, we'd like to send you five CDs of your choice, absolutely free, if you join our club today."

F: **"Hmmph, I wasn't born yesterday."**

S: "Uh—I can understand your concern. But millions of people have joined our club, and—"

F: **"Yeah, sure—millions. Right."**

S: "Yes ma'am. It's because we offer the best product at the lowest prices."

F: **"Says who?"**

This one can be very therapeutic. It's like paying back all of the people who've taken advantage of your trusting nature over the years. The key is to never give an inch. Just keep on challenging and doubting the solicitor's sincerity until he cracks.

The Security Scam

DEGREE OF DIFFICULTY

☎ ☎

TECHNIQUE: Fend off the solicitor with a quick security check.

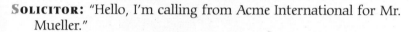

E X A M P L E

SOLICITOR: "Hello, I'm calling from Acme International for Mr. Mueller."

FUNSTER: "Your password?"

S: "Pardon me? Uh, as I said, I'm with Acme International, and I'm—"

F: [*Insistently*] **"Sir, your *password*?"**

S: "I may have misdialed. Is this not 911-555-4321?"

F: [*Press two buttons on your phone.*] **"We have a Code Yellow on line four . . . [*Pause*] . . . Affirmative. Initiating trace."**

S: [*Solicitor hangs up.*]

If the solicitor surprises you by holding on and trying to talk, just alternate pressing the 6 and 7 buttons on your phone (not too fast) to give the sound of an alarm.

The Recording Routine

TECHNIQUE: Evade the solicitor altogether by simulating one of the telephone company's annoying recordings.

E X A M P L E

SOLICITOR: "Good afternoon, this is Janice with a courtesy call from Acme Financial Associates. Is this Ms.—"

FUNSTER: [*Whistle three tones, each a tone higher than the preceding one*.] **"To make a call, please hang up and dial again."**

S: [*Solicitor hangs up.*]

For added laughs, if the solicitor calls right back, whistle the tones in reverse order before giving the message!

By the way, if you don't know what the tones sound like, just take your phone off the hook and listen. In about thirty seconds you'll hear the three tones and some kind of recorded message.

And if you're not too good at whistling, just press the 1, 5, and 9 buttons on your phone in sequence. It won't sound exactly right, but it will be close enough to get you through the exercise.

The Haggling Hustle

DEGREE OF DIFFICULTY

TECHNIQUE: Resist the solicitor by attempting to negotiate everything he says.

E X A M P L E

SOLICITOR: "Good evening—Elizabeth Dixon?"

FUNSTER: "Well, it's a *fair* evening, and you've reached *Liz* Dixon."

S: "Yes, of course. Well, Ms. Dixon, I'm Jason with Acme Diversified Corporation. I'm calling to notify you that you've been chosen to receive our gold card with a $10,000 credit limit."

F: "Hmm . . . [*Pause*] . . . make it $12,000."

S: "Oh, I'm sorry but the limit is—"

F: "Let's come back to that one. Next?"

S: "Uh, well—our introductory rate is only 7.9 percent for the first six months."

F: "I'll take, uh, 6.9 percent for, uh, *eight* months."

S: "Ma'am, I don't think you understand. I can't—"

F: **"Look, you're making this awfully difficult. I'm bending over backwards here."**

S: "I think you'll find this to be an excellent offer. Now, may I send you our gold card? It should arrive within two weeks."

F: **"How about ten days? And I don't like gold—too showy. Do you have silver?"**

The goal here is to make it clear that there's no such thing as a win-win situation. If the solicitor keeps trying, just start asking for totally unrelated perks, such as frequent-flyer miles or free software.

The Just-a-Moment Juke

TECHNIQUE: Psych out the solicitor by repeatedly bringing the wrong person to the phone.

E X A M P L E

SOLICITOR: "Hello, is this, uh, Calvin Parks?"

FUNSTER: **"Oh—no, just a moment."** [***Put the phone down and wait a few seconds.***] **"Hello?"**

S: "Yes, Mr. Parks?"

F: **"Uh, no—just a moment."** [***Put the phone down and wait a few seconds.***] **"Hello?"**

S: "I'm trying to reach Calvin Parks."

F: **"Parks? Oh, hold on one moment."** [***Put the phone down for a few seconds and then repeat the exercise.***]

There are two ways to execute this technique. You can either use your normal voice each time, or you can use different voices. And if you go more than two rounds, you can vary the phrase: "Hold for a moment," "Wait just a second," and so on.

The Phone-Sex Phoniness

TECHNIQUE: Faze the solicitor by giving a response he isn't expecting.

EXAMPLE

SOLICITOR: "Hello, may I talk with Fred Schwartz?"

FUNSTER: "Let's see, pal—hold on a sec . . . [*Pause*] . . . Okay, the only male on staff right now is Rod Manly. He's \$3.50 a minute, unless you like it rough, and then it's \$3.75 a minute. Will this be Master Card or VISA?"

S: [*Solicitor hangs up.*]

With this one you probably won't get any verbal response, not even an "Oh, I'm sorry, I must have dialed the wrong number." The satisfaction comes from a believable delivery. So make it sound like you've said the line a thousand times before, like it's just another day at work.

The Mumbler Morass

DEGREE OF DIFFICULTY

TECHNIQUE: Leave the solicitor guessing about his progress with responses that become increasingly incoherent.

E X A M P L E

SOLICITOR: "Good evening—Ms. Talbot?"

FUNSTER: "Uh-huh, thiz-iz-miz-dabot."

S: "Uh, well, this is Bob Adams with Acme Waterproofing. How are you doing this evening?"

F: "Oh, noz-zo-bad-i-guess."

S: "That's great. Now, Ms. Talbot, you may not be aware of this, but water damage to a basement can cause thousands of dollars in damage."

F: "Well, thaz-a-problem-idon-need."

S: "Pardon me?"

F: "I zed das-sa-promma-ida-nee."

S: "Uh—well, uh, I can understand your concern. Now, if I might . . ."

Don't be surprised if the solicitor presses ahead as if everything is normal. But if he does say he's having trouble understanding you, just mumble more loudly.

BONUS POINTS: To add a little more confusion, you can give a little laugh after one of your comments, as if you've made a witty one. See if the solicitor laughs along with you.

The Surrealism Subterfuge

DEGREE OF DIFFICULTY

TECHNIQUE: Daze the solicitor with a response that would make sense only in the Twilight Zone.

E X A M P L E

SOLICITOR: "Uh, yes, hello. May I please speak to Mr. or Mrs. Reeves?"

FUNSTER: "Oh, I'm sorry—no one's home right now."

This is one of the simplest techniques, but certainly one of the most satisfying. If all goes well, there will be a pause of three to four seconds. Then expect some incoherent babbling as the solicitor tries to come up with a response that makes sense.

But if the solicitor tries to be clever and says "Well, *you're* there, aren't you?" here are some possible responses:

• "What do you mean by 'there'?"
• "No . . . [*Laugh*] . . . I don't *think* so!"
• "Just until I gather up the jewelry and silverware."

And if the solicitor asks "When do you think they will return?" you can say "Oh, they never left. They're just not home right now." If the solicitor then asks what you mean, just say "What do *you* think I mean?"

The Stammer Stunt

TECHNIQUE: Hinder the solicitor with responses that take an uncomfortable length of time to get out.

E X A M P L E

SOLICITOR: "Good evening—may I please speak with Bob Everett?"

FUNSTER: "S-s-speaking."

S: "Mr. Everett, I'm Aaron Fowler at Acme Financial, the debt-consolidation folks."

F: "D-d-debt c-c-c-consolida-da-da-tion. Well—that's, uh—that's—n-n-not a bad, uh—i-i-idea."

S: "Uh—you're right about that, sir. It's all about simplifying your life. Now, may I ask: Do you currently use more than one credit card?"

F: "W-w-well, I've g-g-g-got a M-m-m-master Card, and a V-v-visa, and, l-l-l-let's see—oh yeah, an Amer-americ-c-c . . ."

Remember to take . . . your . . . time! And as the conversation progresses, experience more and more trouble getting your words out. Patience is a virtue, and this is your opportunity to help a phone solicitor become more virtuous.

The Jabberwocky Jerk-Around

DEGREE OF DIFFICULTY

Technique: Confound the solicitor with made-up words.

E X A M P L E

Solicitor: "Hello—am I speaking with Mr. Henderson?"

Funster: "Yes."

S: "I'm Ms. Petersen with Acme Insurance Company. How are you this evening?"

F: "Oh, a little *grebulous*, but otherwise fine—and you?"

S: "Huh—oh, fine. I'm calling with an offer for a free insurance checkup."

F: "That sounds quite *predatial*. Tell me more."

S: "Well, we'd like to meet with you to find ways to save you money on life, home, and car insurance."

F: **"It's certainly an *ediferous* offer. But I'm sort of a *clemiant* person. So can you *eluvirate* your offer a bit?"**

S: "Uh, I, uh . . ."

Give yourself a pat on the back if the solicitor asks what one of your words means. Then you can say "Am I not speaking English here?" or "Well, if you don't know, I'm certainly not going to tell you!"

It's hard to improvise nonsense words on the fly, so it's a good idea to keep a list of them by the phone. Here are a few to get you started:

• ezulient
• brelundity
• defantic
• madiginous
• bartitious
• grolience

The Malady Manipulation

DEGREE OF DIFFICULTY
☎ ☎ ☎ ☎

TECHNIQUE: Bore the solicitor with excruciating details about your health problems.

E X A M P L E

SOLICITOR: "Good afternoon—I'm trying to reach Ms. Jackson."

FUNSTER: "This is she."

S: "I'm Cathy calling from Acme Consumer Research. How are you today?"

F: "Oh, better than yesterday. It's the bursitis, you know."

S: "Oh, well, I see. Now, Ms. Jackson, we're conducting a brief survey—"

F: "It's been acting up lately. But it's mainly when I—have you ever had bursitis?"

S: "No ma'am. Now, I was about to say that we're conducting a survey—it should just take a couple of minutes."

F: **"Well, minutes can seem like hours when you're in pain. But I shouldn't complain."**

S: "If this is a bad time, I can—"

F: **"Now the hemorrhoids—that's a different story. But they're not so bad as long as I put that cream on twice a day."**

S: [*Solicitor hangs up.*]

The solicitor will most likely bail out after a few rounds. But if not, just keep complaining until she says something sympathetic. Then you can say "Well, it's none of *your* business!" and hang up.

To add to the fun, make sounds of discomfort and pain during the conversation.

The Non-Sequitur Neutralization

TECHNIQUE: Bewilder the solicitor with responses that just don't seem to make any sense.

EXAMPLE

SOLICITOR: "Good evening—could I speak to Mr. or Mrs. Bauer?"

FUNSTER: "Yes, but nevertheless."

S: "Yes, well, I represent H and R Acme, the tax return specialists."

F: "After the fact, of course."

S: "Yes sir, and we have a special offer for people who really hate doing their own taxes."

F: "Game, set, and *match*."

S: "Absolutely. And for a limited time, we'll complete your tax return, including all related forms, for only $69.95."

F: "Time and time again."

S: "Um—yes. Well, I think you'll agree that the fee is very reasonable considering the peace of mind you'll get from putting your tax return in the hands of professionals."

F: **"It's neither here nor there."**

If the solicitor ever asks "What do you mean?" just reply with another inappropriate phrase.

Here are some more you can try:

- "As far as the eye can see."
- "Full steam ahead."
- "Kids say the darndest things."
- "And so forth and so on."
- "Just business as usual."
- "Quid pro quo" or any other foreign phrase.

The Intonation Interference

DEGREE OF DIFFICULTY

TECHNIQUE: Baffle the solicitor with inexplicable changes in volume, pitch, and length of words.

EXAMPLE

SOLICITOR: "Hello, may I speak to Mr. or Mrs. Little?"

FUNSTER: [*In a high voice*] "This is . . . " [*In a low voice*]
" . . . Misterrrrrr Little."

S: "Good evening, sir. My name's Barbara, and this is a courtesy call from Acme Eternal Rest Products."

F: "Acme E—ter—nalllllll Rest Pro—ductsss."

S: "Yes, sir. Although it's sometimes difficult to talk about, we all need to plan for our funerals, so we won't be a burden to our loved ones."

F: [*Softly*] "Yes, yes, yes." [*Loudly*] "That is im-por-tant, very important, extreeeeeeeemely important."

S: "Our company has been serving the tri-country area for over thirty years, and our commitment to service is unsurpassed."

F: *[Slowly]* "Yes—yessss." *[Very fast]* "I know your reputation well."

S: "Sir, if this is a bad time, I could—"

F: "Noooooooooooo! This—is—a great time . . . " *[In a high voice]* " . . . to call me."

With this one, be sure your speech starts out just a little different from normal, then gradually make it stranger and stranger. If the solicitor asks if anything's wrong, just answer in your normal voice: "No, nothing's wrong." Then continue with the strange voice until the solicitor hangs up.

The Come-On Connivance

DEGREE OF DIFFICULTY

Technique: Unsettle the solicitor with flirtatious remarks.

E X A M P L E

Solicitor: "Good evening, may I speak to Mrs. Yancey?"

Funster: "Speaking. And you are?"

S: "I'm Mr. Blane with Acme Warranty Extension Service."

F: "Hmm—has anyone ever told you that you have a nice voice?"

S: "Oh, well, thank you. Uh, I'm calling because our records show that your original refrigerator warranty is about to expire."

F: "You sound very strong. Do you work out? I do, three times a week—and it shows, too."

S: "Uh, yes ma'am. Now, Mrs. Yancey, our company is prepared to—"

F: **"Oh, you can call me Sue."**

S: "Certainly. Now, our company—"

F: **"What are you wearing? I've just got on a T-shirt."**

The solicitor will probably hang up before too long. But if he happens to "test" you by playing along, just get more and more explicit with your questions until he cracks.

The Just-the-Facts Jive

DEGREE OF DIFFICULTY

TECHNIQUE: Duck the solicitor's pitch with a series of basic questions about her company and its services.

EXAMPLE

SOLICITOR: "Good afternoon, Ms. Carpenter?"

FUNSTER: "Yes."

S: "My name is Latonya. I'm calling on behalf of the Acme Corporation, and I'm—"

F: "Hold on a sec—let me get a pencil. [*Pretend to be writing.*] "Okay, Ac-me Cor-por-a-tion. And what do you sell?"

S: "We offer financial solutions to—"

F: "Fi-nan-cial so-lu-tions. I see. And where are you calling from?"

S: "Uh, I'm calling from our headquarters in Ottumwa, Iowa. Now, I'd like to—"

F: "Ot-tum-wa, I-o-wa. Got it. And your phone number there?"

S: "Our phone number? Uh, it's 1-800-555-4321. You see, we're—"

F: **"All right, one–eight–hun–dred–five–five–five–four–three–two–one. Okay, thanks, that's all I need right now."** [***Hang up.***]

With this one, the solicitor will expect the investment of time and patience to lead to an opportunity to deliver the pitch. As if!

Bonus Points: Imitate Jack Webb.

The What-If Whitewash

TECHNIQUE: Wear down the solicitor with a tedious series of hypothetical questions.

EXAMPLE

SOLICITOR: "Good evening, Mr. Dawson?"

FUNSTER: "Yes. And you are?"

S: "I'm Ms. Lang with Acme One Credit, and I'm calling to let you know that you've been pre-approved for our Big Card. And we're prepared to waive the initial fee of $25."

F: "And this card is good for any type of purchase?"

S: "Yes sir."

F: "What if I bought a stereo?"

S: "Any purchase under $5,000 is already approved."

F: "Well, what if I have a question about my account?"

S: "Mr. Dawson, you can call our Customer Service department twenty-four hours a day, toll free with any specific questions."

F: "What if there's a war or something, and I can't mail my payment on time?"

S: "Well, all of the conditions are explained in the package that we'll be sending you."

F: "And what if I die prematurely—do I still have to pay my bill? And what if it's a gruesome death versus, say, an accidental food poisoning?"

If the solicitor, for some inexplicable reason, doesn't hang up after a few rounds, you can start to veer off the subject with your questions. For example:

- "What if Custer had used a B-52 bomber?"
- "What if elephants could talk?"
- "What if Bruce and Demi had stayed together?"

The Confusion Con

DEGREE OF DIFFICULTY

TECHNIQUE: Stonewall the solicitor by mistaking his product or service for another.

E X A M P L E

SOLICITOR: "Hello, may I speak to Mr. or Mrs. Crenshaw?"

FUNSTER: "Yes, this is Wes Crenshaw."

S: "Mr. Crenshaw, this is a courtesy call from Acme Roofing Company."

F: "Oh yeah—you're the ones with that commercial that has the two dogs that talk—it's funny."

S: "No sir, that must be some other company."

F: "Oh."

S: "No sir, we're the number-one name in home roofing products."

F: "Oh yeah, now I remember. You've got that Olympic skier as your spokesman. He's very good."

S: "I'm afraid you've got us confused with another company. But I assure you, we're the best in the business."

F: **"You're the folks with that thirty-year guarantee, aren't you?"**

S: "Well, no sir. We do offer a ten-year limited warranty, however."

F: **"Oh. But the free Internet access—you're still offering that, aren't you?"**

Other comments you can make include references to senior-citizen discounts, pricing plans, and store locations. And if you get stuck, you can always double-check a previous exchange: "Are you *sure* you don't have the commercial with the talking dogs?"

And if you decide to bow out early, just say "You don't seem to know very much about your own company" and hang up.

The Who-What-Where Wheedle

DEGREE OF DIFFICULTY

TECHNIQUE: Thwart the solicitor by gathering factual information using only *wh—* words.

EXAMPLE

SOLICITOR: "Hello, could I please speak to Ms. Zimmerman?"

FUNSTER: **"Who?"**

S: "Ms. Martha Zimmerman?"

F: **"Why?"**

S: "Well, I'm with Acme Investment Counselors, a full-service financial planning company offering mutual funds and other investment opportunities."

F: *"Where?"*

S: "Uh—well, our main office is in Omaha."

F: *"When?"*

S: "Ma'am? When what?"

F: *"Whaaaat?"*

You'll probably get through only two or three exchanges before your responses start to make no sense. But if the solicitor insists on pressing ahead and wasting his time while you have fun, then who are you to question his judgment?

BONUS POINTS: Once you've mastered this one, you'll want to try the advanced version (degree of difficulty = ☎ ☎ ☎ ☎). Here you have to use less common *wh—* words, like *whence, wherefore,* and *whither.*

The Here-They-Come Hoodwink

DEGREE OF DIFFICULTY

TECHNIQUE: Bring the solicitor's intended victims tantalizingly close, and then make them vanish.

EXAMPLE

SOLICITOR: "Good evening, may I speak with Mr. or Mrs. Owens?"

FUNSTER: "Oh, they're not here right now. They're—oh wait. I think that's them pulling into the driveway. Can you hold on a sec?"

S: "Sure."

F: [*Pause*] "They're parking now. . . . [*Pause*] . . . May I ask why you're calling?"

S: "Yes sir. I'm with Acme Fence Company, and I'm—"

F: "Okay, they're walking up the sidewalk now. Acme Fence Company?"

S: "Yes sir. And we're having our semi-annual—"

F: "Hold on—they're coming in the door. You still there?"

S: "Yes, I'm still here."

F: "Okay, here they—uh. Oops, sorry—that's not them."

S: [*Solicitor hangs up.*]

Timing is important here. You have to imagine the couple actually parking, walking, opening the door, et cetera. Make the time pass realistically.

The Digression Diversion

DEGREE OF DIFFICULTY

TECHNIQUE: Disarm the solicitor with a mind-numbing reminiscence or anecdote.

E X A M P L E

SOLICITOR: "Hello, have I reached Mr. Vickers?"

FUNSTER: "Yes."

S: "This is Mr. Hill, and I represent the Acme Cruise Line in beautiful Miami, Florida."

F: "Miami? My grandpa went to Miami once. He was a salesman, you know. Women's undergarments. You're not selling women's undergarments, are you?"

S: "No sir, we operate America's most popular cruise ships."

F: "Yeah? Well, he was in Miami in '87—not on business, you understand. No, he was there for a vacation. Oh, and a little gambling. He liked playing the horses, you see. Such a bad habit, don't you agree?"

S: "Well, I—"

F: **"You see, he was a widower at the time, and, well, he still had this health, but . . ."**

With this one, you'll want to keep giving the solicitor small openings, but quickly interrupt and continue with your little story.

Here are some other ways to get your story going:

- "Well, I've never been *there*, but I did go to . . ."
- "You know, I saw a program on Miami on the Travel Channel the other night, and they . . ."
- "Oh, I don't see how people can live there—I mean, the humidity! Now, Los Angeles—there's a great . . ."

The "Misty" Machination

DEGREE OF DIFFICULTY

TECHNIQUE: Put the solicitor on hold and force him to endure an easy-listening classic.

EXAMPLE

SOLICITOR: "Good afternoon—may I speak with Mrs. Salazar?"

FUNSTER: "Sure—can you hold on for a second?"

S: "Yes ma'am, I'll hold."

F: [***Tap a button on your phone, then start humming "Misty."***]

S: [*Solicitor hangs up.*]

If you don't care for "Misty," you could try "Feelings," "People Who Need People," or any Barry Manilow tune.

And if you can't carry a tune, an easy alternative (degree of difficulty = 🕾 🕾) is to actually record a brief segment of a song on your digital memo recorder, then play it into the phone at the appropriate time.

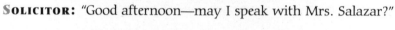

The Indecision Inveiglement

TECHNIQUE: Neutralize the solicitor with an agonizing inability to decide how to respond to the simplest question.

E X A M P L E

SOLICITOR: "Good evening, could I speak to Mr. or Mrs. Goldstein?"

FUNSTER: "Well, they, uh—how should I put this? They're, uh—it's kind of hard to—let's just say they're—no, that's, uh—you see, they—well, I'm just not sure if I should . . ."

S: [*Solicitor hangs up.*]

It's unlikely that the solicitor will hold on for more than a few seconds. But if he does, eventually wrap up your little monologue with something along these lines:

- "Well, to put it bluntly: They're just not here."
- "Heck, I'll just come out and say it: They're not home right now."
- "Uh—I need some time to think about it." [*Hang up.*]

But Seriously . . .

Despite the Fun you can have with phone solicitors, some people may actually want to take steps to reduce the number of unwanted calls they receive. So here is some useful information about telemarketing calls and your options for dealing with them.

The Problem

How do so many companies get your phone number? There are two ways your number can get into circulation (prepare to be surprised).

First, your personal information, including phone number, is routinely sold to telemarketing firms by banks, telephone companies, credit card companies, and other businesses. Telemarketers can buy phone lists organized by age, marital status, income, and many other factors.

And second, whenever you call a toll-free number (800, 888, or 877), your own phone number is made known to the company paying for the call. And there's nothing to prevent such companies from sharing your number with other companies.

So if you want to keep your phone number relatively private from this day forward, here are two important steps to take:

1. Call your bank, credit card companies, and mortgage company and ask that you be placed on their "Do Not Sell" lists. Make it clear that you don't want them giving or selling your personal information to other parties.

2. Call toll-free numbers from a pay phone to avoid making your home number known. Or you can call companies at their regular business numbers. (You'll pay for the call, but you'll be protecting your privacy too.)

The World of Telemarketing

Unfortunately, your phone number is probably already "in the system" and thus available to phone solicitors. Here's how they use your number.

Calls from telemarketing companies are often computerized: The computer dials many numbers simultaneously and waits for a connection to be made. Then it checks to make sure it hasn't reached a fax or answering machine. Then the call is passed to an available telemarketer, who brings your name up on a monitor and enters it into a sales "script." Now you know why there's often a noticeable pause and some clicks before anyone ever talks to you.

Despite the illegality of this method of reaching consumers, it happens all the time. So if you get such a call, try to obtain the solicitor's company name, address, and phone number. Then call your local phone company and report the details of the nuisance call. Under the Telephone Consumers Protection Act of 1991, the phone company is required to investigate.

What to Do

Here are some steps you can take to discourage repeat calls and reduce the number of telemarketing calls you get:

1. Ask for the solicitor's company name and phone number, and write them down. Then ask that your name be put on their "Do Not Call" list. Of course, this action will stop calls only from that one company—and there are lots of companies out there.

2. Write to the Direct Marketing Association and request that you be excluded from telemarketing promotions (ironically, you'll have to give them your phone number). Any telemarketing firms that belong to the Association will eventually get the message. The address is Telephone Preference Service, c/o Direct Marketing Association, P. O. Box 9014, Farmingdale, NY 11735.

3. Increase your understanding of the problem and its possible solutions. Use the Internet to find information about nuisance calls and your legal rights. If you're using America Online, you can type in the keyword *Telemarketing* to get lots of useful information.

A Final Word

Although you can't eliminate all unwanted calls, you can reduce their number. It's just a matter of diligence and common sense. Regardless of what steps you take to preserve your privacy and peace of mind, always keep two rules in mind:

1. Never buy anything from a phone solicitor.

2. Never give or confirm any information about yourself or your family over the phone.

And remember the old adage: If it sounds too good to be true, it probably is.

Official Submission Form

What's your favorite way to deal with obnoxious phone solicitors? Send us your technique, and it might end up in the next edition of *Fun with Phone Solicitors*. If we use it, you'll get credit for submitting the idea and receive a free copy of the book!

Mail to: Robert Harris
c/o Warner Books, Inc.
1271 Avenue of the Americas
New York, NY 10020

Name of technique: _____

Technique: _____

                _____

                _____

                _____

Example:

    SOLICITOR:

    FUNSTER:

    SOLICITOR:

    FUNSTER:

Your name: _____

Your address: _____

                _____

Name of technique: _____

Technique: _____

_____

_____

_____

Example:

    SOLICITOR:

    FUNSTER:

    SOLICITOR:

    FUNSTER:

Your name: _____

Your address: _____

_____